WARTIME WORCESTERSHIRE

Jeff Carpenter

Brewin Books

First published
by Brewin Books, Studley, Warwickshire, B80 7LG
in September 1995

Reprinted November 1995

ISBN 1 85858 058 7

British Library Cataloguing in Publication Data.
A Catalogue record for this book is available from the British Library

Typeset in Garamond and Printed by
Heron Press, Kings Norton, Birmingham B38 9TS

CONTENTS

Foreword
by
The Bishop of Worcester

The Bishop's House
Hartlebury Castle,
Kidderminster,
Worcestershire
DY11 7XX

DIOCESE OF WORCESTER

I feel honoured to be asked to write a preface to this book *Wartime Worcestershire*. For any who can remember the Second World War it is compulsive reading and written by one who patently has an affection for his county.

Those who are younger will find themselves reading important social history. Not least will they discover why their parents and grandparents are unable to forget the wartime years. Everyone, but everyone, was involved. There was full employment, a sense of participation in a high enterprise, taking us all out of ourselves with no room for grumbling. Many were the human stories both poignant and sometimes plainly funny. Villages and towns which in peace-time were sleepy found themselves the scene of enterprises of national, even international importance. No wonder the bells rang and there was dancing in the streets when the final achievement was made.

Why does war, with such degrading and devastating objectives produce such enviable singleness of purpose? How could we recover that with a better end in view - a world at peace and peace founded on justice. However, read on!

Yours sincerely,

+ Philip Worcester

Chapter 1

WARTIME WORCESTERSHIRE

After the armistice in the First World War people were almost wildly optimistic. In the streets of Worcester exuberant girls dressed themselves up in soldiers' uniforms and youths banged on drums and old tins. Sadly by September 1939 that had all been forgotten. Once again the peace was shattered and everyone wondered what lay ahead. The poet John Betjeman had compared Worcestershire to "a diamond shaped fruit tart". Would it be like that after the war or would enemy planes and tanks reduce much of it to a rubble? Even though the full horror of modern war did not descend, the next five years were to prove stirring and eventful times in the life of the County.

The Armed Services

For many who 'joined up' there was action in every part of the world and the task of maintaining the County's proud record from World War One. It was natural that some of the first time soldiers should find themselves in the territorial units of the Worcestershire regiment. These were hastily reassembled and trained at the time of Munich in 1938. They were then thrown into the most brutal sector of war in 1940 ready to meet the full brunt of the heavily armed German offensive against Northern France. The roads were blocked by civilian refugees and there was continuous strafing from the Luftwaffe. "A baptism of fire", wrote General Gale "but one of which they can feel justly proud".

Again in North Africa the 1st Battalion of the Worcestershire Regulars having initially routed the Italians in Eritrea were then struck by the might of Rommel's armour in the epic defence of Tobruk. After this the tide of war turned more favourably with 'the Worcestershire's' making an important contribution to that process. After D. Day Worcestershire regiment units were active in the allied push towards Germany and their capture of Mouen was praised "as one of the slickest attacks of the war". Further along the line inside Germany, the First Battalion became engaged in a fearless attack which captured the village of Tripsath "the most deliberate operation we had yet done" (Major D.Y. Watson). At the other end of the world two other battalions were engaged in the savage South East Asia campaign. One of its notable features was a gruelling forced march of 400 miles from Chindwin through a land of jungle and mountains.

The 67th Field Regiment Royal Artillery more colloquially known as "The Worcester Gunners" had an extremely active war - Belgium in 1940, Tunis in 1943 and Anzio in the same year. Their colleagues in the Worcestershire Yeomanry rapidly abandoned their cavalry tradition first for tanks and then for parachutes. In June 1944 as 'paras' they played a critical role in D. Day and were later involved in the Ardennes campaign and in the airborne crossing of the Rhine.

In the war on sea and in the air there was ample evidence of a vigorous contribution by those who hailed from Worcestershire. The clearance of the beaches at Dunkirk in 1940 and the organisation of the famous Pluto pipeline in 1944 were carried through by the indomitable naval commander, William Tennant of Upton. Similarly the raid on the Tirpitz, one of the most dramatic aerial attacks of the war, was carried out by a Worcestershire flying ace, Vernon Cheeseman.

Preparing Worcestershire For War

On the Home Front, it was known an attack could come at any time. Detailed arrangements were drawn up for each part of Britain and reinforced by a set of strict regulations dictated by the Central Government in London. Lord Dudley, the Regional Commissioner, in conjunction with the police Special Branch was as powerful as an official in the Victorian days of the Indian Empire.

Emergency Order 504 stated that anyone could be drafted to do any task "needed for meeting enemy action". That meant the police could detain any person regarded as suspicious including "campers, secret signallers and corrupters of the public morale". In the event of an enemy occupation we know from evidence about a resistance cell based at Peopleton that there were certainly plans in the County for fighting back. Invasion had to come first. If that happened suspected enemy agents like those members of the British Union of Fascists known to be living in the Evesham Parliamentary Division would have been packed off to Norton Barracks or Gloucester Prison.

Locally the time of greatest tension must have been around 28th March 1941. On that date a set of new orders went out into Worcestershire from the office of the Regional Commissioner.

"ARRAS - A state of extreme tension exists with parachute landings at dawn and during moonlit nights as well as sabotage very possible".

From 1939 the evacuation trains were scheduled to bring Birmingham or London children out to reception centres like Kidderminster, Kempsey, Worcester and the villages. At the same time war workers from as far away as Scotland were also moving in and had to be found accommodation. This often meant strange digs and sharing a double bed with some stranger you did not much like.

All areas prepared themselves to resist bombs, gas, tanks and paratroopers. Lessons were learned the hard way from the shambles of 1940 in Northern France where the roads had been clogged by fleeing civilians. This time the civil defence, police and Home Guard were briefed in elaborate detail about what to expect. Nonetheless a false alarm at Bewdley in June 1940 showed how easy it was to create a shambles. Eight witnesses imagined that they had just seen two German parachutists drop. As a result the order was given for the church bells to be rung and the main streets in Bewdley and Stourport were filled up with sightseers.

If the worse had come to the worst it was probable that the control of the war would be moved up to Worcestershire from London. Chief Constable Lloyd Williams M.C. was required by the Cabinet office to make Hindlip Hall, Bevere House and Spetchley available on immediate alert. Rumour had it that the King and Queen would be going into Madresfield Court where they could have been near neighbours to Queen Wilhelmena of Holland at Croome Court. Certainly there were plans for the Admiralty to come to Malvern where the science block at Malvern College would have become the central signal station for Britain's battle fleet.

Three Important Locations

As war settled in, the work of certain organisations became especially significant. At Wood Norton near Evesham the BBC set up their famous listening unit staffed by linguists who monitored a wide range of enemy broadcasts all around the clock. Their reports were rushed down to London each day and became an essential element in the allied intelligence network. Later on in the war Wood Norton broadcasting was the main vehicle for getting information about food and nutrition over to the British housewife.

Wartime Droitwich was one of Britain's top 'wireless' stations in an era when the radio was central to ordinary life. The Home Service beamed on a 391 wavelength was the major source of news and information. There were also many entertainment and comedy programmes. North Worcestershire's own Ken Horne appeared on the wartime comedy classic, Much Binding in the Marsh and Syd Carter of Wickhamford presented homely chats on the exploits of the local Home Guard. By 1944 another giant Droitwich mast was sending out coded broadcasts to resistance fighters in Europe as well as the celebrated "Voice of America".

In 1942 TRE* with its 2500 scientists moved up from Swanage for security reasons. Suddenly Malvern became a key centre for wartime scientific research. It is hardly exaggerating to claim that the station's brilliant practical results created a wartime legend. In particular Malvern developed a new generation of radar technology which helped the allies to go onto the offensive. The bombing war, the D Day attack and the strike back against U boats were all part of the success story. To get through some of the practical problems it was necessary for the applied scientists, to work closely 'with the top brass'. Thus for quite a while the Commander of the Pathfinder Bomber force was stationed at Defford Airfield. There were also regular Sunday morning think tank sessions at TRE where Air Vice Marshall Tait might turn up as well as Churchill's head of research, 'the Prof', Lord Cherwell.

†In fact there were two boffin establishments in Malvern. The other was R.R.D.E. at Pale Manor which worked particularly on the application of radar for army use especially to improve the accuracy of the big guns. Not far away at Earl's

* Radio location - Telecommunications Research Establishment
† Radar Research Development Establishment

Croome in the grounds once laid out by Capability Brown, army gun specialists tried out the practical aspects of this research. It was no coincidence that an Earl's Croome expert, Major Youensen, was on Monty's staff at the time of the Normandy landings to advise on gunnery matters.

The Enemy Bombers Arrive

The bombing of Worcestershire when it came was light by Coventry standards but certainly not inconsiderable. By July 1942 the County had been hit by 778 high explosive bombs. There were also 8077 incendiaries or *brandbombe* often dropped on open countryside to fire the farms. The worst year by far was 1940 when the enemy began to go for the Midland's industrial targets. Worcestershire was also on the flight path for the many aircraft on their way back from Merseyside to the Luftwaffe bases in occupied France. Specific harassing attacks or 'Storflug' probably came from Stab 1 KG 77 base at Laon. From occupied Normandy targets like Redditch, Bromsgrove, Kidderminster, Stourport and Worcester were deliberately focussed because they were key sites for industry and supply. In 1941 'Jerry' became more concerned about bomber airfields which explains the Heinkel attacks in the Pershore area in the March and July of that year.

A Landscape of Camps and Airfields

As in many other parts of Britain the local landscape soon filled up with camps and airfields. Some were temporary like those for the traumatised troops sent into Worcestershire after Dunkirk. One such camp lay along the Avon riverbank on Evesham Meadows where the locals seemed shocked to see British lads in such a state. Others were training camps like that for crack Free French troops at Ribbesford near Bewdley - the elite St Cyr military academy in exile. After escaping from Dunkirk, the headquarters staff of the Belgian Army were installed at the Abbey Hotel in Malvern. Also in the Malvern area there was a high ranking contingent from the Polish Navy as well as Dutch soldiers and Dutch airmen. The publisher, Harry Batsford who decided to set up in Malvern for the duration of the war noted how certain of the locals were convinced that the muscular French speaking Canadians doing P. E. exercises on the common were German spies operating a concentration camp.

In addition there were huge hospital camps - home to 79000 U.S. wounded servicemen in Worcestershire and Herefordshire. Finally there were the compounds for German and Italian prisoners. These seem to have been moved around as space became available. At certain times there were POW's at Hampton Lovett, The Chateau Impney and Blackmore Park. Italian prisoners were required to help on the farm front in the Vale. We also know that by 1945 a number of the Germans at Honeybourne Camp were not happy about repatriation back to the Soviet Zone. They had a leader called Mufti and were regarded as highly industrious by the camp commandant, Captain Forster. One of them was using modern equipment left behind by the Yanks to provide a dental service for some of the local inhabitants.

Airfields

At the beginning in 1940 there were the scatter fighter airfields all over the County - part of Command Group 2 covering the Midlands and east Anglia. By May 1942, as the tide turned the bomber bases at Pershore, Defford and Honeybourne were increasingly important. In 1942 Defford previously only a small station, became the official home of the Telecommunications Flying Unit and thus intimately linked to the top research base at Malvern. From here planes took off on the big and often controversial raids on Europe equipped with the latest devices. With an increasing number of airfields in operation there were also many many unfortunate and often grisly crashes. A police incident book for Pershore covering 1942 refers with sickening regularity to one crash after another. One highly dramatic fighter crash occurred at Madresfield in 1941 when a brave Polish pilot, Franek Surma steered his faltering Spitfire away from exploding right onto Malvern. Two years later on 29th May 1943 Wellington Number X3704 went out of control during a fly past in the Pershore Wings For Victory Week and all five crew members were killed. Hitting the roofs and chimney pots in Bridge Street, the plane took the top off the Brandy Cask Hotel before crashing into the back gardens aligning the River Avon.

The Industrial Front and The Farming Front

Worcestershire's economic contribution in these years deserves much wider recognition. A bigger county then, its industries were at full tilt throughout the war. The Black Country chainmakers of Cradley and the puddlers of Wilden and Netherton worked long hours of hard labour. An historian of Redditch has described how they turned out "guns, guns, guns" as well as the light motorbikes which were crated up and frequently dropped by parachute to help the allied armies. Austin Aero Engines were at Cofton Hackett outside Bromsgrove, one of the several County factories specialising in vital aircraft production. ICI at Summerfield near Kidderminster made large quantities of ammunition. Royal Arsenal at Worcester were similarly engaged as were the former Kidderminster carpet factories now converted over to war work. In the far north just outside Halesowen the tubemakers, Steward and Lloyds were responsible for the fabrication of Pluto, a crucially important supply pipeline for petrol used at the time of the D Day landings. At Malvern, the small but significant firm of Malvern Aircraft claimed to have produced 73 miles of essential tubing for Cromwell tanks at the time of El Alamein.

There was also a wonderful effort in agriculture - Digging for Victory was not just about allotments, 120,000 acres being brought back into agricultural use. Farmers, advisors, and volunteers sided by 2000 Land Army girls helped in the

Exercises to Prepare the County for Bombing

monumental task of clearing the brambles and putting down some rudimentary drainage.

Voluntary Organisations

The voluntary organisations were crucial to the war effort and almost everyone seemed to get involved in one way or another. That formidable figure of wartime broadcasting, Mable Constanduros, claimed that there was one unnamed doctor's wife from Worcestershire who was working harder than anyone in Britain.

The ARP got stuck in early in 1940 as the bombs started dropping on Redditch, Frankley, Kidderminster, Burcot, Stourport, Malvern and Worcester. At this time NFS and AFS units were also racing up the road to deal with the blitz in Coventry, Birmingham or further afield to London, Bristol and Plymouth.

Some duties were harrowing. The AFS hated going out to clear up after plane crashes. In 1940 it was usually young fighter pilots in training and in 1942 more likely the bomber crews especially in the Pershore area. Other voluntary duties were just long and boring, but extremely important for all that. The petrol tanks at Stourport were Category A "vulnerable points". Like many others they had to be given specific round the clock protection.

Another "drag" was observer duty - keeping a constant eye out for bandit aircraft from the high spots like Bredon Hill or Broadway Tower. From these observer points relevant and often valuable information about enemy aircraft movements was telephoned in and immediately plotted onto the giant RAF intelligence maps.

Problems and Pleasures of Everyday Life

There was a powerful human side to the Home Front War. It appears as fascinating and complex today as it was then. Thousands of outsiders were drafted into Worcestershire as key workers with the authorities having powers under Order 504 "to secure" their billets. We have to imagine the difficulties of implementing this in a free country. Sir Bernard Lovell was suddenly landed in Malvern as one of 2500 scientists needing accommodation and described his first 'digs' as "a dark cavernous, depressing house with hostile people".

At Evesham a massive influx of BBC staff took place a week before the outbreak of war with the town's billeting officer operating from the coal order office on the end of Platform One of the railway station. The new BBC residents were won over by the beauty of the place and prepared to put up with slight problems. Beryl Cleare was allocated to accommodation where she shared a double bed with a spiritualist woman who talked all night.

Women had a busy time of it in the war. The lasses at RAF Pirton were amongst those having the chance to learn significant new skills working on aircraft navigation equipment. In Worcester all the pay and pensions of the RAF (involving millions of transactions each week) was handled by a highly efficient and predominately female clerical staff. Equally capable women clerks at Droitwich (Salvage D Department) carefully recorded all the weapons captured.

By the standards of earlier times women's wages were not too bad. In 1943 factory girls in Kidderminster or Redditch were earning about £2/14 (£2.70p) and paying about 15/- (75p) a week at home for their keep. It was the housewife who also normally organised rationing for the family. By 1942 that extended far beyond the original basic items bacon, meat, butter and sugar. The result was a lot of time waiting in queues.

During these years Worcestershire people also became prodigious savers both of money and materials. In Kidderminster Alderman George Eddy was an example of those who pushed National Savings with a fanatical enthusiasm. All the main towns set themselves ambitious targets to buy fighters and bombers for the war effort. Worcester in one year collected 28 tons of bones for high explosive glycerine. Out in the deep countryside at Astley Hall even Stanley Baldwin, a former Prime Minister, was requested to sacrifice his famous wrought iron gates for melting down into scrap.

Entertainment certainly did not die. A good deal of the interest centred on the County's 42 cinematographic halls, as they were described. They ranged from smart new Odeons to the Temperance Hall in Lye. We can imagine the excitement when Clark Gable, star of that wartime epic Gone with the Wind, led a contingent of US officers from Wolverley Hospital Camp for a night out at The Gliderdrome, Kidderminster's best known hotspot.

Dancehalls were regarded as the best places for visiting servicemen to meet the local girls. A 1944 Bromsgrove Messenger offered five different week night dancing venues. For a 3/- entry there was the No 5 Platoon Dance at All Saint's Parish Hall with the "Pop Band of the Midlands" or The Red Cross Dance at Bromsgrove Parish Church Hall with Fred Reynold's - entry 3/6d.

Some increase in crime was to be expected, given the general pressure of life during wartime. Many of the offences were petty. Aircraftmen stationed in Pershore certainly had a penchant for making off with pushbikes. At Evesham much to everyone's surprise three unfortunate Birmingham evacuees were hauled up before the magistrates for stealing plums.

A few of the wartime cases had a much higher profile. Two murders achieved particular notoriety - the Bella Skull Mystery at Hagley and the murder of Florrie Porter at Lickey. This latter unsolved case caused considerable local alarm among young women. It involved a popular Bromsgrove typist who was stabbed to death after going out with a G.I. officer.

Some of the black market crime also aroused interest. In June 1942 the Master of the Croome Hunt was accused of a widespread misuse of army lorries and their drivers for his own private contracts. It was also claimed he had ordered expert army mechanics off their official tasks to do kennel duties for the hunt.

One of the most bizarre of all black market frauds occurred at Honeybourne Camp. The U.S. hospital camp personnel not only pulled out abruptly but left behind an estimated £8 million in equipment - enough to furnish six field hospitals. Locals who knew what was going on reported that new surgical equipment, long lines of refrigerators and mounds of new sheets and towels lay scattered throughout the camp. As a result questions were asked in the Commons and the ensuing court case filled the scandal columns of the News of the World.

Education at War

Worcestershire education in 1939 was of good repute but strongly traditional with a high proportion of private schools. The State sector tried to adopt a selective tone where possible. The headmaster of King Charles 1 Grammar in Kidderminster "is assisted by a staff of University graduates and others", announced Kelly's Directory.

For many of the County children it meant elementary school with large classes and with their regular teachers gone off to the war. Hopefully the position was slightly better than that experienced by George Randall a few years earlier in 1936. The future Leader of Worcester Council was asked to leave Kemerton R.C. School at the age of thirteen to make room for a new pupil aged five.

As for the schoolchildren, by no means all were in good health. Town centres were often rat infested (104,151 were cleared from Worcester during the slum clearances of the 1930's). In 1938 a prominent 'medic' labelled Worcestershire as a T.B. black spot and this view was confirmed by the existence of sanatoria or hospital isolation units at Bromsgrove, Dudley, Evesham (Bengeworth), Knightwick, Kidderminster, Pershore, Ronkswood and Upton.

When the bombing came in 1940 it was decided to move many of the private schools out. At the opposite end evacuees were coming in to swell the ranks of many little County primary schools. In Kempsey village the head was landed with an additional sixty nine pupils and the next week was asked to fix up accommodation locally for 120 delicate children from Uffcombe Open Air School in Birmingham.

Neither was life easy for those moving out. Malvern College boys were comparatively fortunate in being exiled to the marble splendours of Blenheim Palace. The Malvern Girls College moved to three different stately dwellings in Somerset where the electrical wiring worked spasmodically and the face flannels froze hard in the washbasins overnight.

By the end of hostilities all schools had made some kind of contribution to the war effort. The youngsters from Samuel Southall, a school serving a deprived area of Worcester collected so much scrap, that it was claimed part of the school looked "like a salvage depot". Worcestershire schoolchildren also sent toys to their bombed out counterparts in Birmingham and Coventry. The greatest sadness was concerned with former pupils who never returned. Hanley Castle, the smallest grammar school in the County lost eighteen. Kings and the Royal Grammar in Worcester between them lost one hundred and nine.

Peace Comes Again.

As the conclusion of war became obvious people naturally began to think of the future. Incidentally it was at a 1941 church conference at Malvern that Archbishop

William Temple had made one of the first serious contributions to the debate about post war reconstruction and the welfare state.

At last in 1945 the peace returned in Europe if not the Far East. Events at Malvern on V.E.Day reflected the jollification everywhere. Giant searchlights made Victory V signs in the nightsky the church bells rang out and there was dancing in the streets. The symbols of light and fire seemed to be uppermost in people's minds. The towers of the parish church were illuminated at Kidderminster and Evesham. In the countryside huge areas of gorse were fired at Castlemorton and Suckley and there were big bonfires at Stourport, Bewdley and Droitwich At the County Ground, New Road, cricket started up again with the old favourites Perks, Howarth and Jackson now reinforced by some promising new talent; Singleton, Jenkins and. Palmer. People rejoiced to see the lads and lasses come home. By good fortune Worcestershire had escaped what Richard Baxter once called "the calamitousness of war". But it had earned its share of grief and won more than its fair share of achievements*

*.*One of the survivors was the poet, W.H. Auden Auden left Worcestershire as a prep school master to fight in the Spanish Civil War. Before leaving and with characteristic generosity he organised a proxy marriage with a German Jewess just to get her out of Nazi Germany So the story goes the good lady stepped off the train at Great Malvern went up to the nearest man, and asked "Excuse me are you my husband ?"*

Chapter 2

END OF ONE WAR BEGINNING OF ANOTHER

The County's Main Memorial Piled High With Flowers

Sorrow for the fallen was keenly felt after 1918 as shown by this early photograph of the memorial outside the Cathedral.

Woodbine Wille

The War To End All Wars

Women's Tribute Day, August 16th 1919 was only one of many processions in a wild celebration of peace throughout the county. Fred Inight recently demobbed, noted the scene in Worcester "In continual rain - many people in the town dancing, singing etc., Crowds rather rowdy towards midnight. Many girls dressed in soldiers' clothes. Children marching in parties through town beating tins etc.,"

WOODBINE WILLIE, THE WORCESTERSHIRE WAR CHAPLAIN - ON THE WAR TO END ALL WARS.

Studdert - Kennedy was surely one of the 1914-18 heroes. In this poem written in cockney slang he explored the sentiments of the ordinary Tommy after the armistice. He claimed it was necessary to see beyond all the bogus celebration and realise the true horror of the trench war that had just ended.

"To my Comrades - the best men in the world!

Well that's not what I went out for
I'm not one o' them as swanks.
I don't want no celebrations
Nor no earty votes of thanks.
I'm not wantin' beer and beanfeasts,
Nor no buckets of soft soap
I've 'ad bigger things to deal with
And I''ve seen a larger 'ope.
I went out for Right and Justice,
I went out to fight for Peace,
Not a patched up thing on paper
But lasting true release
Of the people from the madness
From the scheming and the lies
That end up in bloody murder
And the useless sacrifice
Of the very best and bravest
That our mothers bore in pain
From the piles of broken bodies
Lying rotting in the rain".

G.A. Studdert - Kennedy. (Fragment of a longer poem)

A Famous Exile From Fascism

Haile Selasse, Emperor of Abyssinia is seen here at the 1924 Wembley Exhibition. After his country was invaded by Fascist Italy in 1935, the Emperor with an entourage of 16 servants lived until 1941 at Blakedown House, Belbroughton.

Baldwin - The Arch Appeaser?

A charge against Baldwin is claiming "that dictators only understood the language of force" whilst "addressing them with the language of good will and reason" (Corelli Barnett)

Official barriers often prevented Jewish Exiles from Nazi persecution settling in Britain. Despite this a group of Austrian Jews found refuge in the Pershore area. Hans Cohn, an Austrian Jew found a warm welcome at the Worcester Blind College. With no German specialist on the staff, the Headmaster, B.O. Bradnack instructed that initially he should be taught in Latin.

Laurence Housman

Born in Bromsgrove and brother of the more famous A.E. Housman. As a Christian writer and internationalist he represented the well intentioned but naive body of opinion which would not countenance another war at any price. Once the war started however, Laurence Housman gave strong support to the plans for reconstructing a fairer and juster society once it was all over.

The Bishop's New Neighbours

Bishop Perowne living at Hartlebury Castle in 1938 suddenly found a huge RAF arsenal springing up nearby .... The RAF established 7 centres comprising a storage space of two and a quarter million square feet in the quiet hamlets of Elmley Lovett and Rushock and Hartlebury. The creation of Maintenance Unit 25 involved a major defence decision to house many of the RAF's spare parts deep in the Worcestershire countryside on a heavily disguised site. The components were packed and despatched to all war zones by a staff of 3000.

The Admiralty Never Came

If London was severely bombed the 1939 war plan made arrangements for the Admiralty to move to Malvern. Winston Churchill as First Lord would have been at School House and the Preston Science School would have been the chief signal station for controlling the British Fleet. Happily this never came to pass. Instead the navy came here in the form of H.M.S. Duke, one of Britain's largest training establishments. By V.E. Day 80,000 recruits had been trained on the large site in St Andrew's Road. As the local newspaper reported there were more jack tars walking around Malvern than most British sea ports.

Chapter 3

PREPARING FOR INVASION

For Evacuees - The Magic Of The Worcestershire Countryside

These youngsters are out amongst the hopfields at Suckley. For some, this was an experience which established a lifetime's love of the countryside. Jean Ward was just eight when she was evacuated from Birmingham explained how she often went to the Malvern Hills on the bus "We had great fun there tobogganing on sheets of cardboard. We would go blackberrying and I can remember filling shopping baskets there were so many. Auntie (her foster mother) bottled them, made jam and made lovely blackberry and apple suet puddings".

Jean Ward and Friends

Evacuees Looking Around A Great Worcestershire Building.
Jean Ward's foster parents were very kind but firm. When the billeting officer brought her and her sister to Prince Rupert Road there was a lovely tea - chocolate and marshmallows. "We still wet the bed for a time but she was very patient with us. - we were never in the front room nor upstairs except to go to bed (it would wear out the carpet)".

The Worcestershire Miners' Home Guard

No 15 Platoon was recruited to defend Bayton Colliery - surely the smallest coalfield in Britain. Only 23 in strength it was armed "with pick helves or other suitable weapons".

Clifton Home Guard Watching Over Rural Worcestershire

The Home Guard put in long hours over all the wartime years. Many of the County's road crossings took on a blighted appearance when the Home Guard created them into defence areas. That meant concrete tank obstacles, high entanglements of barbed wire and trenches.

Worcester ARP At The Ready

The County and City ARP Units were organised separately from 1938. If crisis came the tasks were awesome. People had to be rescued from bombing, the use of gas had to be anticipated, shelters allocated as well as the constant watch out for invading bombers.

The Well Sandbagged Shelter At Kidderminster Town Hall

These soldiers with gas masks might have needed them if they got inside some of the town's concrete shelters. In 1943 Council debate, Councillor S. Goodwin complained that they were so insanitary and smelly that townsfolk would sooner risk the bombs. The Mayor angrily insisted that every shelter had certainly been cleaned out once by the NFS in the past four years.

Kidderminster in 1938

Kidderminster became a busy town during the war. Carpet factories like Tompkinsons were converted over to ammunition production and with the influx of war workers the population went up by ten thousand. Because Kidderminster was an important industrial target there were 6 bomb attacks and 620 air raid warnings including a famous occasion when the enemy dropped some bombs by parachute.

Bewdley June 1940 - Church Bells For A False Invasion Alarm

The period after Dunkirk was one of mounting tension all round. One day a message came through to the Bewdley Home Guard that German parachutists had landed in Ribbesford Woods. The report was backed by eight witnesses including two "reliable policemen" so the officer in command decided to ring the church bells - the sign of general alarm. A military screen was thrown around the woods and a bren gun carrier scuttled over from Norton Barracks. The woods were searched but no parachutists were found. It was said that freak air currents had blown bales of hay into the air after an aircraft flew over. The streets of Bewdley and Stourport were blocked with crowds of curious pedestrians. It was an occasion when the Home Guard learned a lesson or two.

Evesham In The 1940's

After Dunkirk there was a transit camp on Evesham Meadows with wounded soldiers resting in the park along the Avon. On the old bridge itself there was a heavily barricaded checkpoint.

Halesowen At War

Note the air raid shelter entrance in the foreground of the picture. Halesowen appears here as a historic village but within its outskirts was a prime enemy target - the Stewart and Lloyds tube works.

Resistance If There Was A Nazi Occupation

The secret resistance organisation for the West Midlands included Lewis and Edmund van Moppes two emigre diamond merchants living at Wolverton Hall near Peopleton. Later newspaper reports claimed that the brothers would have exercised a key role in organising the sabotage units for undermining any German military control in the area

The Big Houses

Hindlip Hall - Churchill's Refuge If Things Went Wrong?
If Napoleon had landed in 1805 George III would have come from Windsor to Hartlebury Castle. If Hitler had landed in 1940 possibly a main centre of the government operational network would again have been in Worcestershire. In 1939 the Secretary of the War Cabinet was in direct communication with the County Chief Constable to ensure that RAF personnel would evacuate Hindlip Hall at 24 hours notice. The code word Melbourne meant "protect Hindlip, Bevere and Spetchley".

Chapter 4

BOMBING

The Attack On Meco

One of Worcestershire's worst bombings came on October 3rd 1940 when 7 were killed and 64 injured. At the time the Meco was producing important aircraft parts. One of the bombs fell at an angle carving its way through a machine shop wall and causing a huge blowback.

Barrage Balloon Over Earls Croome

These huge monsters were tethered to steel cables. They forced enemy bombers to fly high so their attack would lose accuracy. This balloon was probably to protect the gunnery research station here.

Bombing on Malvern

This devastation was a result of some of the bombs which fell on Malvern. They came down on Yatesbury Road, Somers Road and Pickerleigh Road but missed a main target, the railway line at Malvern Link. In 1940 an enemy pilot thought he would crash into the hill behind the town. He dropped a load of bombs into Wyche Cutting in an attempt to lighten his load and gain height. Apart from the bombing, it was claimed that wartime Malvern took on an austere character. The streets were cluttered with auxiliary water pipes and static tanks and the buildings fronted with ugly sand bags.

Secret Bunkers Near Kidderminster

Kidderminster had 6 bomb attacks and 620 air raid warnings but these secret shelters at nearby Wolverley were for some deeper purpose. Set underneath woods and farmland they were entered through a series of tunnels.

Heinkel Bombers Over Pershore

This was the type of German raider used to try and wipe out the new bomber airfield near Pershore. Sixteen high explosive bombs fell in a direct attack on March 16th 1941 and on the following July 5th another 10 H.E.'s and 100 incendiaries fell on neighbouring Bishampton (the craters are still visible).

Chapter 4

THE ARMED SERVICES

Bearing The Brunt Before Dunkirk

The two territorial units of the Worcestershires hastily assembled and trained in 1939 met the full force of the German armoured attack in Northern France. The roads were blocked by refugees and there was continuous strafing from the Luftwaffe. "A baptism of fire" wrote General Gale "but one of which they can all feel justly proud".

North Africa - The Worcesters In Action

In the Eritrean Campaign the First Battalion routed the enemy at Gogni and Barentu and then held out gallently against the might of Rommel's panzers in the epic defence of Tobruk.

'Rocky' Miles of Droitwich Larking About Somewhere On The Western Front.

A Regimental Signpost between Imphal and Kohimar, Burma

The Worcestershire Regiment Far From Home In Burma.

**The Navy.
Captain William Tennant -
beachmaster At Dunkirk.**

*This "severe and imperturbable
figure in blue" was charged with the
task of evacuating the beaches of
Dunkirk in 1940. No less than
378,000 were rescued in a day and
a half under fierce attack by enemy
dive bombers. Later after surviving
the sinking of HMS Repulse, he was
in control of the Mulberry Harbours
and Pluto at D.Day.*

A Worcestershire Attack On The Tirpitz

*So important was the Tirpitz to German prestige that Hitler forbade her to put to sea if there
was any danger. A Worcestershire naval pilot won the DSO leading a famous aerial attack on
the battleship.*

An Enemy Body Illustrates The Vicious Fighting In Burma

"Grimmest tenacity" - that is how the Japanese General Fujiwara described the final stages of the Burma War in which the Worcestershire Regiment figured so prominently. The campaign involved the famous struggles for Imphal and Kohima. Also the 400 mile forced march from the Chindwin River.

A Mobile Canteen at the Anzio Beach Head

The big amphibious assault at Anzio involved a number of Worcestershire soldiers serving with the 67th Field Regiment of the Royal Artillery. It was tough fighting in which the opposition used 'the Anzio Express', a huge German railway gun 215 tons in weight with a range of just under 40 miles.

Tiger Moth, G-ARTL

Many types of aircraft flew from Worcestershire's "scatter airfields". Whitelys from Honeybourne and Bothas from Halfpenny Green. Tiger Moths of this type were used to train pilots at the No 2 Elementary Flying School operating from Perdiswell. It was a dangerous job involving low flying instruction in the air corridor along the Severn between Worcester and Upton. It was necessary to avoid two sets of high tension cables as well as the telephone wires near Upton Bridge. Landing at Perdiswell was also not without its difficulties. The shape of the airfield was described "as a distorted burgundy bottle". The only flying aids were a wind sock and a flag. For night flying the markers for the landing path were some goosenecked paraffin lamps.

Worcestershire Pilots in Front of a Tiger Moth

By 1940 this county was an integral part of Britain's vital air defences. Worcestershire was in Command Group Number 12 guarding the East and The Midlands. From a number of "scatter airfields" such as Perdiswell, Halfpenny Green, Pirton and Honeybourne a variety of aircraft took to the air.

Worcestershire Part of Fighter Command Group 12

Drawn by J.Williams

A Wellington

These became the pride of Pershore and Defford Airfields. As early as 1940 Wimpeys the Builders were under orders to start constructing a bomber airfield at Pershore on the Throckmorton Racecourse. The initial purpose was to train aircrew and at Pershore they were soon able to put 27 bombers a night into the air. By 1942 these airfields were actively participating in the bomber attacks against Germany.

Loading a Cylinder Dambuster Bomb

In March 1943 Squadron 617 made a famous attack against Eder Dam. One of those who perished in this bold and dramatic episode was Squadron Leader Henry Eric Maudslay of Fox Hill, Broadway. Henry Maudslay had trained as a pilot in 1940 and was shot down with his crew during a direct attack on the dam.

Chapter 5

WORCESTERSHIRE'S KEY LOCATIONS

MALVERN

A.P. Rowe - Pioneer Of Air Defence

The Superintendent at TRE, A.P. Rowe (Jimmy Rowe) is seen here with the Royal Party. Rowe had been involved in air defence problems from the outset in 1934. He was one of the earliest to realise that the increasing speed of military aircraft made defence by anti-aircraft batteries hopelessly inefficient. Unfortunately other methods like locating enemy aircraft by sound detectors were little better. A.P. Rowe became secretary of the famous Tizard Committee on which some of the most brilliant scientific minds in Britain discussed out the best methods of defending Britain against enemy aircraft. At Malvern, Rowe assembled a formidable team of experts including six fellows of the Royal Society.

Royal Visit To TRE

The visit of King George and the Queen was an official recognition of the vital work done during the war at RSRE. The research unit with 2500 staff moved in from Swanage in 1942. Fearing a commando style attack at Swanage, the removal had to be accomplished with dramatic swiftness. The equipment and staff were installed within a week during which it poured with rain.

Pathfinder Bennett At Defford Bomber Base

There were daunting practical problems associated with H2S (an offensive radar technology for bombing) and it took Air Vice Marshall D.C.T. Bennett to organise the solutions. As the "greatest flying expert in Bomber Command and the Commander of the newly created Pathfinder Force", Bennett was ordered to Defford, the nearest bomber field to T.R.E. Malvern. He remained there until the airbourne trials for the project were completed. His fervent belief in H2S was without doubt a critical factor.

Top Brass At Malvern

One of the high level meetings held at Malvern between service chiefs and Britain's leading applied scientists. It became a habit to meet on Sunday mornings for what were termed 'Sunday Soviets'. The vital scientific problems of the war were discussed in a completely free and informal atmosphere with no holds barred.

A Defford Airfield Plane Equipped With The Latest Malvern H2S Scanner (see the perspex Cupola on the underbelly). Defford started life as a mere satellite field to Pershore. By May 1942 it had officially become the home of the Telecommunications Flying Unit. This linked Defford to all the top secret research work a t Malvern

Blind Firing From Bombers Against Enemy Fighters - A Result Of Malvern Research.

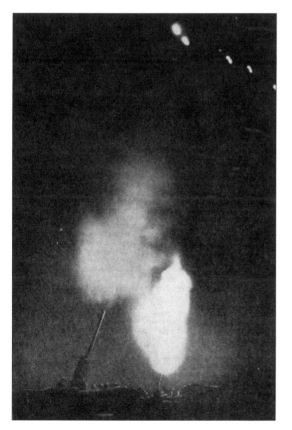

Earl's Croome, Where Science Came to the Aid of the Gunners

A Centimetre - Wave Radar on a Twin Bofors Gun Mounting.
It was Worcestershire research which made Allied gunnery more accurate again by the application of radar. Amongst the apple blossom at Earl's Croome the military worked closely with Malvern boffins in one of the key units of CAEE (Coast and Anti-Aircraft Experimental Unit). The skills developed were of considerable importance during the allied advance and Major Youens from Earl's Croome was a leading gunnery expert on Monty's staff. Radar was also used by CAEE scientists to improve searchlights. Their invention was given the colourful title of "Elsie".

You see, Doctor, I bin doin' 12 uhr -Shifts

Self Portrait of Someone Overworking at Wood Norton

"I bin doin' 12 uhr shifts doctor" reads the caption of this cartoon by the poet, Geoffrey Grigson. Other colleagues made transmissions of the broadcasts which were then rushed away to allied intelligence units by motorcycle couriers.

Wood Norton Home of The British Monitoring Service
They set up the BBC's listening post a week before war commenced. In the M. Unit hut amongst the trees of the Wood Norton Estate, enemy broadcasts were monitored twenty-four hours round the clock. The staff were a highly dedicated if eccentric band of linguists. For security reasons they were ordered not to advertise their presence in the town and described themselves as "civil servants".

BBC DROITWICH

Syd Carter of Wickhamford and Childswickham Broadcasts to the Nation

Sent out via Droitwich were Syd Carter's wartime talks on the Worcestershire Home Guard. As well as the Home Service the station also put out a special Force's Programme on its own 20 kilowatt transmitter.

Droitwich's Giant Mast - Bringing You 'The Voice of America'

The new 300 foot self supporting mast constructed with Lend- lease funds in 1944 was so powerful that overseas broadcasts sometimes bounced off cast iron drain pipes in the neighbouring Wychbold area. The BBC European Service and The Voice of America sent out from Droitwich were essential elements in getting the Allied message over to occupied Europe.

Radio Entertainment from Droitwich

These were vocalists with the Skyrockets radio dance orchestra. Their fans using any make of radio could tune into the Droitwich transmitter. Droitwich beamed the Home Service, the main British station on 391 metres. It brought news and information as well as entertainment.

Chapter 6

INDUSTRY FRONT AND FARMING FRONT

Cradley's Chain Works

Many of the huge chains used on Britain's warships were made in Cradley. Valentine Noake watched them being made in the 1940's in sheds "where half-naked giants wield hammers and the air resounds with the clanging blows".

Halesowen and D Day

Pluto (Pipe Line Under the Ocean) was the huge steel pipe line for carrying across allied petrol supplies across at the time of the D Day landings. The intricate task of laying the pipeline, shown here, was matched by the problem of producing sixty two miles of strong but flexible steel tube. For the Stewarts and Lloyds Tube Company of Coombs Wood Halesowen it was just a question of getting on with 'Job 99'.
Here, a "Conun" is being towed across the Channel and laying a length of steel pipe.

Netherton In The Worcestershire Blackcountry

Charles Knight's powerful watercolour shows a works owned by the family of the former prime minister Stanley Baldwin. During the war Netherton was also the location of Lloyd's Public Proving House where the Royal Navy's biggest anchors and cables were put to the test.

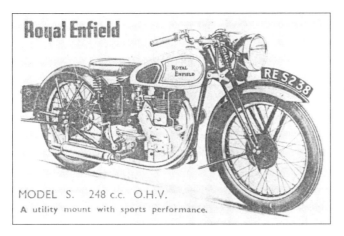

A 1938 248 c.c. Royal Enfield

The lighter model was dropped off in parachuted crates from gliders for the use of the fighting troops below.
As well as Royal Enfield and BSA bikes Redditch factories turned out chromium plating, high duty alloys, batteries, wire drawing and spring coiling machinery. Very important indeed were the Redditch 'shadow factories' manufacturing aircraft components.

British Bullets from Rural Worcestershire

This British soldier firing his Enfield 38 at Arnhem could have been using bullets made at Summerfield near Kidderminster. In 1940 the rural peace of this Worcestershire hamlet ended abruptly with the establishment of a large ICI ammunition factory. The ammunition workers lived in barrack huts at Shenstone and built up an infamous reputation locally for their proficiency in darts, snooker and bingo. By the end of the war the Summerfield buildings had become an important research and development centre for rocket motors.

73 Miles of Malvern Tubes In The Desert War

At the firm of Malvern Aircraft they made the vital sections of tubing for tanks, Hurricane fighters, armoured cars, amphibious craft and M.T.B.'s. Only at the end of hostilities was W.H. Harris, their managing director, able to divulge how the firm had flown out 73 miles of tubes for Cromwell tanks during the key stage of the desert war.

Meco Vital For Its Aircraft Parts and Coalcutting Machinery

This Meco factory in Worcester was so important that after it was bombed in 1940 a telegram came almost immediately from the Minister of Aircraft Production. "Wire back full particulars of deaths and injuries, maximum extent of damage and estimated earliest date of continuation of production".

From Worcester Sauce To Surgical Dressings

It is said that in 1938 Neville Chamberlain took some bottles of Worcester Sauce to The Munich Conference to help put Hitler in a good mood. Four years later the Worcester Sauce Factory was involved in the pursuit of war against the fascist dictator. Sections of the factory were given over to the production of surgical dressings.

No More Milk Delivered By Canal

By 1940 Worcestershire milk was no longer coming into Cadbury's Model chocolate factory at Bournville. Cadbury's canalside works in Worcester also switched over from Dairy Milk Chocolate to producing ammunition for the Royal Ordnance.

Worcestershire's Young Farmers At War

As a major agricultural county things had to get moving. The young farmers were one of the many groups who made their impact felt on the Farming Front. Others like the office girls at Berrows News formed themselves into an allotments club to go out and work the land during their time off.

Winning The War On The Land

Wartime Beauty in The Vale of Evesham
"This was the land of cider, fat bacon and bread pudding" wrote Fred Archer about the Vale in the 1930's. But in 1939 grain was the real farming priority. Worcestershire farmers brought 120,000 acres of land back into use and faced up to the monumental tasks of clearing away the brambles and installing proper drainage.

A Few of Worcestershire's 2000 Land Army Girls

Often they were townies like Lillian Hope an East Ender who hardly knew what a cow looked like. They were trained at Avoncroft and Worcestershire was the first county to open a Land Girl hostel. Someone in a Bredon pub is supposed to have remarked about Land Army girls "they're helluva good looking but they quickly gets the backache dibbing the beans".

Land Army Girls March to Worcester Cathedral

Italian Prisoners of War Help With The Farming

Vera Gardiner was one local girl who married one of the Italian POW's helping on her farm in the Vale of Evesham. At different times there were internment camps at Hampton Lovett and also at Blackmore Park and Honeybourne when the other residents moved away. Some of the Germans at Evesham did not want to be repatriated back to live under Communism. Their right to remain here was supported by the camp commandant, Captain Foster who described them as "grand workers".

Chapter 7

SHORTAGES

Salvage

Scouts happily involved in the national salvage drive for reusable materials. Worcestershire schools also played a major part.

We Collect Anything For The War Effort

In 1943 Worcester City collected 28 tons of bones for high explosive glycerine. The rooms in the Guildhall were "overflowing" with aluminium scrap.

Removal of iron railings from the Shirehall, Worcester

Marching Past The Halifax Bomber Which The Citizens Bought

Wings For Victory Week was celebrated in all the County towns. The government encouraged each town to believe it had purchased outright a certain number of bombers, fighters and warships. It was a part of the powerful savings movement consisting of three hundred thousand individual savings groups all over Britain.

Boffins Queue For Lunch At The Malvern Winter Gardens

The Winter Gardens "was an incredible organisation" wrote Sir Bernard Lovell, "staffed by WVS and serving 1000 people of all sorts - they gave good food, plenty of cheese and butter". In many towns you could also eat in a British Restaurant. At the Public Hall in Worcester's Corn Market you could obtain quite a good dinner for 1/3d (6p) in the hall where Elgar had once played music.

Queuing For Oranges

Ben Bray of Worcester serving oranges to a classic wartime queue consisting of only one man. The headgear of the woman with a shoebox indicates that she is probably a munitions worker. Her hair would be tied up to prevent it becoming entangled in the machinery.

Chapter 8

ASPECTS OF WARTIME LIFE

TRANSPORT

An early view of Worcester's famous engine sheds - part of the County's busy railway network

Many of the familiar GWR locos soon disappeared from the scene on overseas war service. Their vital job of transporting freight and passengers was carried out by LNER tender engines known as Graf Spees. Two of these were kept at Honeybourne "for banking up" the Campden incline.

Canal Scene At Oldbury

The Worcestershire barges had family traditions going back to the historic river trade. In the war the canal network enjoyed a revival. Oil pipelines were still in the future and coal had to be brought down from Cannock to the riverside power stations of Stourport and Worcester...

Crowded Buses In A Wartime Traffic Jam

Buses and trains were the only available transport for many and were invariably crowded. The roads were especially busy with army trucks going to and from places like Norton Barracks or the big camps. In 1940 in an emergency it took two hours for a bren gun carrier to get from Norton Barracks to Bewdley.

WOMEN AT WAR

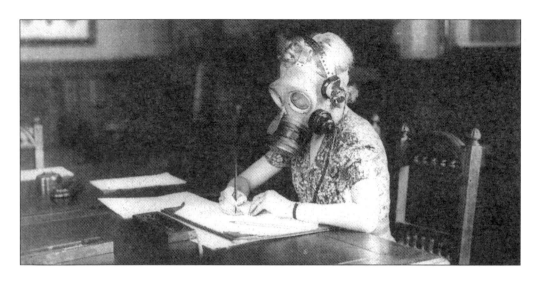

A lady working in the Town Clerks Office in Worcester

Smartly dressed lady with gas mask on Worcester Cross

Her brooch reveals that she belongs to one of the voluntary organisations. Women made a truly outstanding contribution to the County war effort. The Red Cross and the WVS were involved in everything. Their support was especially valuable when Worcestershire became a centre for droves of exhausted and traumatised troops returning from Dunkirk in 1940.

Food Advice For The Nation From BBC Evesham

For four years the Ministry of Food used the Buggins Family programme as a way of giving bewildered housewives food and recipe advice on the 'Kitchen Front'. Grandma Buggins (Mable Constanduros) broadcasting from Evesham was one of the best loved radio personalities of the time. She received a heavy mail bag of enquiries about setting up food advice centres, about fruit bottling and 'Make Do And Mend'.

A Glowing Reference For Worcestershire Womanhood

Mabel Constanduros as a leading broadcaster was asked to do many things - opening Wings For Victory Weeks, Warship Weeks and Salute The Soldier Weeks. Those who earned her highest regard were the women working in Britain's voluntary organisations like the WRVS and the Red Cross. She was especially impressed by a doctor's wife from Worcester - one of those "giving their whole life to war work".

Ladies Sewing For The Troops
These thick socks more than likely ended up at Westwood Park near Droitwich. This was one of the main storage centres for the knitted comforts made by volunteers for the armed services.

Women At War

The WAAFS at Pinvin Camp were employed on important work. By the end of the war many who stayed on were servicing all the important aircraft instruments like compasses and bomb sights.

Fashion and Beauty 1940's Style

A Worcestershire working girl in 1943 could earn about £2.14/- (£2.70p). She would expect to give her mum about 15/- (75p) to live at home and pay 10/- for meals in the work's canteen. Buying Woman's World would cost 3d, cigarettes 2/5d, lipstick 1/1d and the obligatory jar of cold cream for a beautiful complexion 2/6d.

Barbara Lewis Of Suckley As A Landgirl

This attractive wartime youngster borrowed these clothes from a landgirl just for the joy of wearing something different. It was quite understandable because new clothes involved sacrificing scarce coupons with each woman receiving only sixty six in all. A new coat took fourteen coupons and a dress eleven. You even needed coupons for this land girl's uniform.

Women Footballers From The Metal Box 1942

The war brought new opportunities for women both in leisure and work.

50

YOUTH

Practical Training For ATC Cadets In Morse Code And Stripping Engines

The official term for being in the cadets was pre-service training. This was enormously expanded in wartime and cadets went straight into all branches of the armed forces. According to a county handbook for 1946 - "they have done splendid work".

Sea Cadets At Physical Training

This inland county had a reputation for both the quality and quantity of its naval training. At Worcester they trained in an ancient East India hulk. At Malvern there was a huge naval training site, HMS Duke which altogether turned out 80,000 cadets. As the local newspaper reported there were more Jack Tars in Malvern than in many British ports.

Worcestershire Youth At A Wartime Rally

Youth organisations flourished as a way of fostering community spirit and the war effort. At the same time there was concern about the moral welfare of the young. In the Diocese of Worcester there was such a worry about unmarried mothers that six homes or shelters were set up at Malvern, Dudley, Kidderminster and Worcester.

Chapter 9

SOME TEMPORARY RESIDENTS

The Free French At Bewdley

"France has lost a battle but France has not lost the War". At Ribbesford House near Bewdley General Charles De Gaulle achieved the living proof of his famous 1940 proclamation. Ribbesford became the home of the elite St Cyr Military Academy in exile. The 211 officer cadets who played a key role in their country's liberation, were trained in the grounds and nearby Hartlebury Common.

In Training To Liberate France

The Free French cadets seen here in training did not have an easy time. At least a third were to lose their lives fighting to liberate French territory. Living in a number of nissen huts as well as the big house these units published their own Free French journal, 'The White Forage Cap'. There also appears to have been a rather mysterious group of wartime French residents at Pensax Court on the Shropshire border.

A Free Belgian Newspaper

Chateau Impney

John Corbett's French imperial grandeur was turned over to a fascinating range of wartime activities. The rose gardens were turned into workshops, the lawns were covered with huts and the grottoes were used as chambers for testing poison gas. From 1943 to 1945 the house itself was in use as a prisoner of war camp.

Malvern - The Place To See Some Striking Uniforms

Wartime Malvern was like an enclave of free Europe. The French cadets could be recognised by their navy berets and flowing capes. Nearby, residing at the Abbey Hotel were the headquarters staff of the Belgian Army in exile, many of whom had braved great hardship getting into Britain. There was also a small but high ranking contingent of the Polish Navy "engaged on special and secret work". Making up the rest of the town's overseas visitors there were 500 Dutch soldiers and airmen, French Candians and sizeable numbers of invalided G.I.'s.

US Forces Football At St George's Ground, Worcester

The American forces brought style and pace to the local leisure scene. With so many US troops stationed here they tended to take over certain pubs like the Lock Inn, Wolverley. On the music scene they could offer bands like 297 Squad - "14 first class musicians" who played for dances at All Saints Parish Hall in Bromsgrove.

A US March Past In Kidderminster

US troops march proudly past Kidderminster Town Hall. Locals were fascinated by the relatively luxurious life style at Wolverley and the other US Hospital camps. Affluent G.I.'s were warned about "pinching Tommie's girls" but it appears that the Worcestershire girls were usually the ones to take the initiative.

Hospital train

Hospital train Number 15 at Kidderminster station with wounded from the front. Some 79,000 American servicemen were treated in Worcestershire and Herefordshire. There were five US military hospitals in Malvern and two at Burlish near Stourport. American bomber crews and wounded servicemen from the Italian and Normandy campaigns were also sent to camps at Wolverley near Kidderminster and to Bromsgrove. Spetchley Hall outside Worcester was also in use. Amongst the patients were young nineteen year olds traumatised by the brutality of battle experience.

A Worcestershire Writer Observes

Francis Brett Young living in the Avonside Village of Fladbury became acutely aware of an increasing American presence. He described how the neighbouring villages suddenly filled up with trucks driven by black Americans. He noted that in the parish churches congregations had become wildly enthusiastic about singing exotic spirituals.

Chapter 10

EVERYDAY LIFE

CRIME

The G.I. Murder

Florrie Porter (on right) was a popular Bromsgrove girl - a member of the St John's Ambulance, who had once been in a local jazz band. Her mutilated body was found on the Lickey Hills in October 1944. The case provoked a degree of panic amongst young women with American boyfriends. The murder was never solved although it was known that the prime suspect was an unidentified G.I. officer, she had referred to as Hal.

The Bella Murder

In 1943 the police were investigating a dismembered female skeleton found buried in and around a wyche tree in Hagley Woods. The circumstances of the burial at first suggested an ominous witchcraft ritual. A letter to a newspaper written years later claimed that the remains were those of Bella, a spy who had fallen out with her colleagues. Her spy ring had supposedly been sending back intelligence reports to aid German bombers in searching out British factories.

(by courtesy of the West Mercia Police Authority)

A German Spy At Bromsgrove?

File Reference Number P.F. 46476/B2b Klemens Farber born 21.9.1911 at Steinbach was teaching at Bromsgrove School in 1938. The police carefully recorded his particulars and kept a close eye on him. They reported that he toured around on a motorbike "taking photographs which he sends to Germany to be developed". He might still have been around in the Spring Term of 1939 when Bromsgrove School shared a camping expedition with a German youth group. It was reported that on departure one of the Germans harangued everyone with a long speech on the benefits of National Socialism.

A Big Black Market Scandal

These refrigerators were abandoned by the US army and originally dumped at Honeybourne Camp near Evesham. The Yanks left behind scarce and valuable equipment and goods valued at about £8m and enough to equip six military hospitals. The ensuing black market scandal engrossed readers of the News of the World for weeks.
(*Photos by courtesy of the West Mercia Police Authority*)

SCHOOLS

The Worcester Royal Grammar School

Where the Lord Woolton Potato Pie was first sampled. Having given his name to this economical wartime dish, The Minister of Food came up especially to test it.

Education in Exile

The Malvern College site was immediately commandeered for war work and 400 boys moved into the marble spendours of Blenheim Palace. This is one of the state rooms converted into a dormitory.

ENTERTAINMENT

Worcestershire Regiment Lads From Norton Barracks Enjoy Some Time Off

The soldiers also supplemented their income on the black market. The US soldiers from Blackmore Camp near Upton traded Camel cigarettes, coffee and razor blades for fresh country produce brought straight into Blackmore Camp by some of the Callow End farmers..

Hollywood Stars Pop In To Visit

Clark Gable was the famed star of the wartime epic, 'Gone With The Wind'. He came to visit U.S. troops hospitalised at Wolverley. He also called in at The Gliderdome, Kidderminster's hottest 'nightspot'.

Puppets at Malvern

George Bernard Shaw had been present when The Lanchester, Malvern's famous puppet theatre opened in 1936. Later its members came to enjoy a fine war record, touring the country in all weathers from their Malvern base. As a highlight to War Weapons Week or Holidays At Home Week this theatre brought wonderful shows like "Underwater Ballet" and "Circus" to audiences of enthralled children.

Marcel Callow Boxing For ENSA

Marcel Callow (on the left) is seen here in a summertime boxing display outside Croome Court. Marcel also worked for the wartime entertainments organisation, ENSA. This was still the age of live entertainment. Female dance troupes like the Gondoliers, comics, impressionists and above all dance bands got regular bookings at camps and hostels all over the County.

Chapter 11

PLANNING FOR A BETTER TOMORROW

Enjoying The Park - Kids in Gheluvelt Park Worcester
In some ways things got better for the kids. There were now facilities like nursery units, childrens clinics and a special allocation of orange juice. Things had needed to improve. In 1938 the County had been branded a T.B. blackspot by a reputable doctor and there were sanatoria and isolation units at a number of places including Dudley, Evesham, Knightwick, Ronkswood and Bromsgrove.

Victory at Last
This Victory Tea Party was in the yard off Friar Street, Worcester. "I can't remember what was on the table" said Mrs George, one of the organisers. "Everybody found a little because we wanted to do something for the kids. All the families were there; Smith, Facey, Davies, George, Bullock, Milner, Bowers and Granny Smith as well."

HOSPITALS

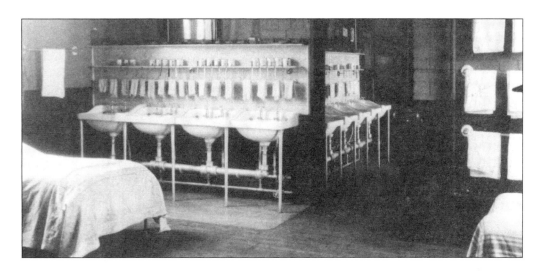

Worcester Royal Infirmary In The 1930's (Courtesy of the County Archives Service)

Medicine locally improved during wartime. A medical historian, Dr McNenemy noted especially the introduction of penicillin, blood transfusions and other new medical techniques. Dieticians, radiologists and other new professional categories appeared in the hospitals and there was consultation with doctors from the many American hospital camps scattered over the region.

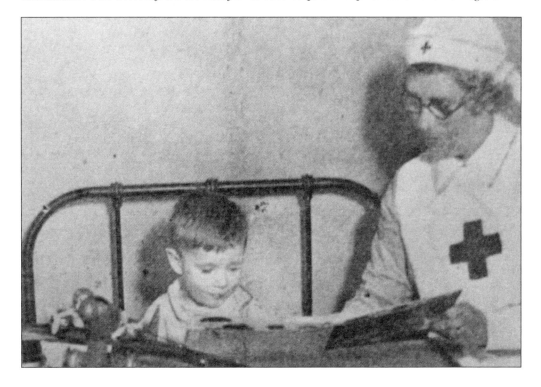

Evacuee In Hospital

HOUSING

In 1944 this lady was still living in a traditional rock house at Wolverley (Courtesy of the County Archives Service)

The Housing Dream 1945 Style

Planners in the County thought this was the future. So did many young couples who had married in wartime and faced a desperate shortage of available properties. One letter to a Malvern newspaper from a top research scientist stated that he was finding it impossible to get anywhere decent for his family to live.

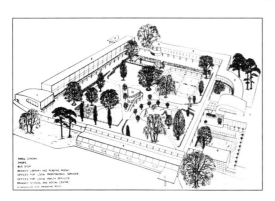

Plans For A Neighbourhood Centre

Post war modernist planning was to become the vogue especially in Redditch. In this integrated scheme for Worcester, the utopian architecture seems ghastly. Yet all the facilities for a civilised life are included: health centre, library, primary school, childrens' play garden and cinema.

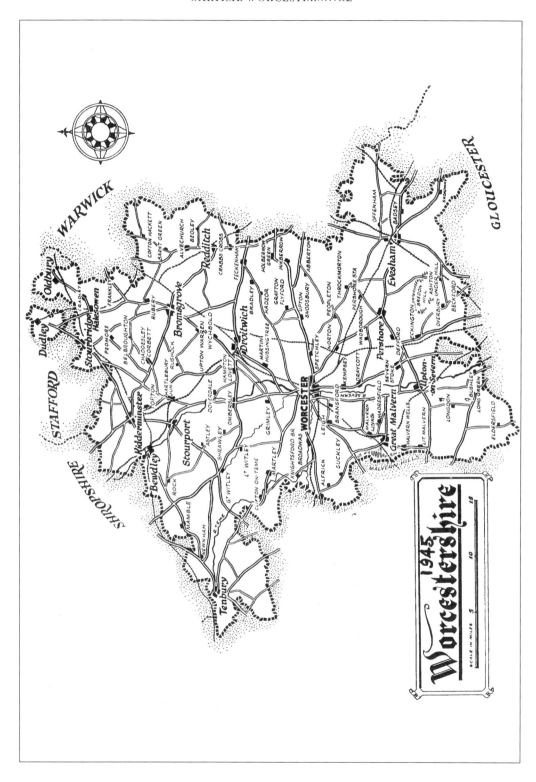

The County At The End Of The War

Overcoming A Tragedy At Malvern

Sir Bernard Lovell, later The Astronomer Royal has described the immense practical problems facing those who were trying to get H2S (an offensive radar technology for bombing) to work amidst all the chaos of moving 2000 scientists into Malvern. The Air Staff had made a categorical directive that the radar should give allied bombers a range of at least fifteen miles. Malvern scientists and engineers from the firm EMI were clearly on their way to achieving this most difficult of tasks and were involved in a short series of trial flights to demonstrate the technical equipment in operation.

On the evening of June 7th 1942 Lovell was given the news that many of his top colleagues had perished in Halifax Bomber V9977 which crashed near Goodrich Castle. Apparently because one tappet nut on the inlet valve of a Merlin engine had not been tightened this tragedy occurred because Lovell was called out to see the bodies of his brilliant colleagues lifeless under sheets near the charred remains of the bomber with the only working equipment on board. He wrote later "It is hardly surprising that I believed this to be the end of the H2S project".

There followed an extraordinary series of events which got H2S back on schedule and ironed out its previous development problems. Summoned to the Cabinet Room in 10 Downing Street the Malvern chiefs were told by Churchill.

"We don't have objections in this room, I must have 200 sets (H2S's) by October". Much of the success which followed was obviously down to Sir Bernard Lovell and his talented colleagues. Fortunately they also had unstinting and dynamic support from at least two other sources. To help the development of H2S, The Commander of the Pathfinder Force, D.C. Bennett was sent to nearby Defford Airbase and practically lived there until the problems had been cracked. Bennett was considered "the greatest flying expert in Bomber Command "and this inexhaustible Australian had such a fervent belief in H2S that his commitment became a critical factor. The scheme had now become so significant that the government appointed one of the leading industrial figures in Britain to be its coordinator for research development and production. Sir Robert Renwick, Chairman of the London County Electric Supply Company gave orders that if Malvern's scientists met any obstructions they were to contact him immediately and he "would phone the PM".

ANOTHER WARTIME OCCASION

Honeybourne Camp -
Black Market On The Grand Scale

In 1945 the US forces pulled out of their 350 acre medical sub depot at Honeybourne near Evesham. It was supposed to be a planned withdrawal but according to later newspaper reports, the Americans left behind £8m in stores, enough to equip six army hospitals. There were graphic descriptions of army huts filled with expensive medical equipment as well as household items virtually unobtainable on the British market like refrigerators and washing machines. All over the camp vast quantities of stuff had been dumped - witnesses spoke of seeing "every known drug", electrical equipment and sophisticated surgical instruments trampled into the mud. Matters were made worse with reports of German POW's dressed in US uniforms piling everything onto great dumps and burning furniture. Some Germans were seen wiping down US vehicles with had towels, pillows and blankets. Mrs Freda Harris who saw all this, reacted like any woman who had been through five years of rationing "The place" she said, "was a housewife's paradise".

This level of temptation meant that crime could hardly be avoided. The soldiers on guard discouraged casual pilfering but they couldn't stop organised corruption. Two Camp officers, Lt.M.C. Herbert and Captain Foster took most of the blame and despite his distinguished war record, Herbert was sentenced to 5 years penal servitude. Two privates, very much the smaller fry in the affair were described by the judge "as thorough thieves and rogues" although they were not sentenced. The receivers of the stolen goods were from South Wales. They brought lorries from the Rhondda Valley to pick up refrigerators and other stolen material at crossroads and other specially assigned locations in the Evesham area.

BIBLIOGRAPHY

The First Battalion, The Worcestershire Regiment in North West Europe.

Major D.Y. Watson. (published by The Worcestershire Regiment.)

The Regional Military Histories. The Central Midlands, Lt. Col Howard Green (Osprey).

Echoes of War, Sir Bernard Lovell (Adam Hilger 1991)

Radar Revealed, Malvern Gazette 1945. Compiled E.H. Pultley

The Radar Army. Reg Batt (Hale 1991)

Worcestershire Home Guard (Courtesy The Worcestershire Regiment and Col. Lawes)

Assigned To Listen, The Evesham Experience 1939 -44

Olive Renier and Vladimir Rubenstein (published by the BBC)

Crime Stalker (published by Central Television)

Shreds and Patches. Mabel Constanduros (Lawson and Dunn)

Droitwich Calling (pub. Droitwich Spa Heritage Centre)

Writers' Gallery. Donald Brook (Rockcliff Publishing)

Worcester Official Guide.   (The Worcester Press)

War Factory : A Report By Mass Observation (pub V. Gollanz)

Dudley. G Chandler and I.C. Hannah (Batsford)

RAF Pershore.   A History. Glyn Warren (published by the author)

Hartlebury. R.O. Walker (pub R.O. Walker)

Diocese Of Worcester. The Church and People In Need. Peter Braby

The Young, The Old And The In Between.   Tom Bainbridge (published by the author)

Kelly's Directory of Worcestershire. 1940 Kelly's Directories

Angriff Westland.   Dilip Sarkar (Ramrod Publication)

Muddy Boots and Sunday Suits. Fred Archer. (Hodder and Stoughton)

The Records of the Worcestershire County Police (By courtesy of the Chief Constable West Mercia Police Authority)

Peter Hennessey. Never Again (Vintage Publications)

Baldwin, A Biography. Keith Middlemass and John Barnes (Weidenfeld and Nicolson

The Deluge. Arthur Marwick (Bodley Head)

Worcester's Memory Lane.   Mike Grundy (published by Worcester Evening News)

Worcester At War.   Jeff Carpenter and Brian Owen (Worcester City Council Museum Service)

Worcester. The City of Things Both Old And New. (The Worcester Press)

An Evacuee In Worcester (unpublished Mss by kind permission of the author, Jean Ward.)

Wolverley Camp Lucy Torode (Wolverley and District Historical Journal Volume 4)

Belgium Unvanquished R. Motz (Lindsay Drummond)

History of Redditch. John Rollins

The Lanchester Puppets. G.L. Somerville. Article in World Of Toys Leslie Daiken (Lambarde Press)

Paul Addison The Road to 1945 London 1977.

E.M. Baker The First Forty years in Worcester. The W.R.V.S. 1938 - 78.

Donald Bell An Experiment in Education.

The History of Worcester College for the Blind: Hutchinson 1967.

Berrow's Journal (published weekly throughout the War).

Angus Calder The People's War - Panther Edition 1971.

J.H. Carpenter, G. Pye and A. McMorrin

History of the Worcester, Co-Operative

Society (Unpublished MSS)

Peter Calvocoressi and Guy Wint, Total War, Penguin 1974.

Michael Craze, TD. MA., King's School, Worcester 1541-1971, E. Baylis 1972.

Alton Douglas, Birmingham at War - Birmingham Post and Mail.

H.V. Follett, A History of the Worcester Royal Grammar School, E. Bayliss 1951.

General Richard Gale, The Worcestershire Regiment, Lee Cooper Ltd. 1970.

Janet Glaisyer et alia, County Town, A Civic Survey for the Planning of Worcester. (John Murray 1946.)

J.G. Hinton, 'Facing up to Hitler', Article Worcester Evening News, Nov 1978.

St. Paul's School Logbook 1939-1945/Gorse Hill, Primary Log Book.

Peter Kirby, The Guiding Wairey Eye, Article for Fly Past.

Denis Walker, Metal Box Limited, Worcester. A History (1980)

Worcester Citizens Handbook of Useful Wartime Information (Pub. Worcester Corporation).

Worcester Evening News (published daily during the War).

Worcester City Civic Exhibition September 1947.

Year Books of the City of Worcester 1930-1945 (Pub. by the County & the City of Worcester).

Frank Huggett, Good Night Sweetheart, W.H. Allen 1979.

Norman Longmate, How We Lived Then. A History of Everyday Life during the Second World War (Hutchinson 1971)

George MacBeth, A Child of the War, Jonathan Cape 1986.

Arthur Marwick, The Home Front, Thames and Hudson 1976.

W.H. McNenemey, History of the Worcester Royal Infirmary.

Henry Pelling, Britain and the Second World War. London 1976.

B.R. Owen Worcestershire Yeomanry Cavalry, a brief chronology - (Worcester City Museum)

Harold Smith, War and Social Change. Manchester University Press 1986.

Henry Sandon, History of Worcester Royal Porcelain from 1862 to the Present Day, Barrie and Jenkins.

Penny Summerfield, Women Workers in the Second World War 1986, Croom Helm

Samuel Southall, Boys Elementary School Journal.

ACKNOWLEDGMENTS

My attempt has been to provide a readable general account of wartime life in our own County.   It is a worthwhile story, previously neglected. With his usual generosity, the Bishop of Worcester agreed to write the preface. That is appropriate because he himself symbolises the community spirit which brought out the best in those wartime years.

Many others have kindly helped both with photographs and information. I particularly acknowledge the assistance of : Barbara Ronchetti, Jane Thorniley-Walker, Ian Rutherford, Helen Sykes and their Colleagues in the Worcester Museum Service, The Staff of the Educational Technology Department at Worcester College Of Technology, Mike Grundy, Gordon Clarke, The Editor of the Evening News, Colonel Lawes of The Worcestershire Regiment, The Chief Constable of the West Mercia Police Authority, Lydia Warner of the West Mercia Police Museum, The Staff of the County Archives Department, John Hewlett and the British Legion, The Staff of the Droitwich Heritage Centre and of all the branches of the County Library Service, The Imperial War Museum, Roy Slim, Marcel Callow -formerly of ENSA and countless others.